REDEEMED

FROM PIMP TO PULPIT
"A LIFE TRANSFORMED BY GRACE"

BY GEORGE (DANNY) HUNTER

Scripture Quotations

ISBN: 979-8-9885131-6-2

Dedication

This book is dedicated to the people who have shaped my life in profound ways:

In loving memory of my mother Hattie Mae Sylvester; and father Clifton Sylvester, and also my biological father George Hunter Sr. To my family: Your unwavering love and presence have been my foundation through every twist and turn of life. You stood by me through the good, the bad, and even the most uncomfortable moments, never wavering in your support. Your unconditional love is truly priceless, and I am forever grateful. Thank you for never giving up on me. I carry your influence, lessons, and love with me every single day.

To my Church Family at New Beginning Ministries: You are more than just a community of believers; you are my spiritual family... Can't forget my Senior Pastor Russell Your love, support, and teaching have been instrumental in my journey to discovering my purpose in God. My Beloved Spiritual Parents Prophet Teresa, Prophet to the Nations, and Chief Apostle Greg, International Apostle thank you for your guidance, wisdom, and unwavering example of faith.

To my Street Family, the brothers and sisters I've walked with in the highs and lows: though our paths have been rocky, you are a part of my story, and I pray my journey inspires you to seek something greater.

To Freedom Transportation, my work family: Thank you for being part of my life and encouraging me in my walk toward better things.

Finally, to the Johnsons, Apostle Monterol, and your lovely Wife Prophet Shalonda thank you for a place of employment. Your friendship and love have been a constant blessing, reminding me daily of God's goodness.

Through it all, God is Good. His hand has been on my life, bringing me from where I was to where I am. I dedicate this book to Him above all, for His endless grace and mercy.

Thank you all for being part of my journey. You have helped shape the man I am today.

Foreword

As a Pastor and Teacher, it is both humbling and inspiring to witness the incredible growth and transformation of Deacon George Hunter. His journey is a testament to God's unwavering love, grace, and ability to redeem and restore those who open their hearts to Him. Deacon Hunter's story is one of perseverance, faith, and the undeniable power of God's calling.

Redeemed is more than a personal testimony—it is a divine proclamation of hope, love, purpose, and grace for anyone seeking freedom and restoration. Through every chapter, Deacon Hunter invites us to reflect on the boundless opportunities God places before us when we surrender our lives to His plan.

This book resonates deeply because of its authenticity and transparency. Deacon Hunter does not shy away from sharing his struggles and triumphs, which makes his story relatable and inspiring for readers from all walks of life. His openness challenges us to confront our own journeys and embrace the redemptive power of God's love.

Each page of Redeemed is filled with transformative truths that will break down barriers, dissolve doubt, and guide readers toward discovering their God-given identity and purpose. Deacon Hunter's story reminds us that no matter how far we may fall from God, His arms are always open, ready to receive and renew us.

This book is a powerful tool for anyone yearning for a fresh start and a deeper relationship with God. It is a must-read that will leave you reflecting on your own journey and celebrating the amazing grace of redemption.

Sincerely,

Sr. Pastor Al Jackson

Destined For Greater Worship Assembly

Table of Content

Acknowledgement

First and foremost, I want to acknowledge my amazing wife, Angel Hunter. You are my everything—my rock, my support, and my greatest blessing. Your love and belief in me have carried me through, and I thank God for you every single day.

To my sisters Judy, Pat, Nette, Tracie, Terrie, Mary (in memory), Christine (in memory), Tina (in memory). Also, my brothers Charlie and Marcell (in memory) each of you has played a unique and special role in my life. Your love, strength, and encouragement have been invaluable, and I'm forever grateful for our bond.

To my daughter Danielle Hunter: you are my pride and joy. Watching you grow into the woman you are today has been one of the greatest privileges of my life.

To my granddaughters Ryan and Ava: you light up my world in ways you'll never fully understand. You are the future, and I pray this book inspires you to pursue a life filled with faith, purpose, and love.

I thank God for each of you and the role you've played in shaping my life and this story. Without your love and presence, this journey would not have been possible. This book is as much a reflection of you as it is of me. Thank you for everything.

CHAPTER ONE

A Child's Journey

Train up a child in the way he should go,

and when he is old, he will not depart

*from it. – **Proverbs 22:6***

My journey began as the oldest boy in a family of ten children—seven sisters and three brothers. Being the oldest boy came with a lot of responsibility, but it also carried feelings of fear and shame. I often compared myself to others, even to my siblings, feeling like I didn't measure up.

We grew up in a busy household. My mother and stepfather did their best to provide for us. While my sisters dressed well, I wore hand-me-downs from the Salvation Army. I learned early to appreciate what little we had, but deep down, I resented being called "poor boy" by my peers. It planted a seed of bitterness and a longing for more.

Our family attended the Everlasting Baptist Church on St. Clair, where I learned about God. My stepfather was strict, teaching us to work hard and do chores. Despite this, I was a shy, fearful boy who got chased home from school. My sister, Pat, often fought for me until the day my father told me to stand up for myself. That day, something changed, and I stopped running.

Though life was tough, there were bright spots. On weekends, we'd go sightseeing as a family, calling it "night riding." We'd laugh, dance, and create memories together. Those times were a glimpse of the joy God intended for families to have.

But even in the church, I struggled. I was a mischievous boy and once stole money from the offering basket. When I got caught, shame kept me away for a time. Still, deep inside, I felt a pull toward something greater. I even dreamed of becoming a preacher, but the streets eventually drew me in.

Fathers, do not provoke your children to anger, but bring them up in the discipline and instruction of the Lord. – Ephesians 6:4

As a teenager, I worked at Pick-and-Pay to help support the family. However, my desire for material things and the resentment of being "poor" led me down the wrong path. By 13, I was stealing and selling joints to fit in. My mother discovered my wrongdoing and warned me, giving me one last chance. She told me, "If you want something, be honest and work for it." Her words stayed with me, even as I ignored her advice at the time.

My relationship with my mother was special. She was my hero—teaching me life lessons, how to treat women, and most importantly, the value of honesty. My mother always stood by me. She helped while I was on the stroll and collected my money when I was away. My mother was a Security Officer and would flash her badge to get me out of trouble with the law: all while trying to convince me to get out of the game. She corrected me when I went astray and always prayed for me, hoping I'd find my way back to God.

Do not be deceived: "Bad company corrupts good character." – 1 Corinthians 15:33

The streets began to influence me. I started hanging out with friends who had flashy cars, nice clothes, and girls surrounding them. I thought that lifestyle was appealing. By 15, I was breaking into houses and getting caught up in crime. My reckless behavior escalated until one night, it all came crashing down.

We were drinking and hanging out when a group of men in army fatigues ambushed us, pointing rifles at me and my friends. I was beaten and humiliated. My mother rushed to the scene, firing a gun in the air to save me. She prayed for me, but I still didn't listen.

*The fear of the Lord is the beginning of wisdom, and knowledge of the Holy One is understanding. – **Proverbs 9:10***

Through all my wrongdoings, God's hand was on my life, protecting me even when I didn't deserve it. I ignored the warnings and the prayers of my mother and kept chasing a life that would only bring destruction.

Though I had moments of clarity, like when I realized I couldn't rob people because it wasn't in my heart, I still allowed myself to be pulled back into the street life. The seeds of faith planted by my mother and stepfather were there, but the weeds of sin and temptation choked them out for a time.

In the chapters to come, I will share how God's mercy and grace reached me in the depths of my despair. From a scared, shame-filled boy to a rebellious teenager, and later a man lost in sin, God never stopped pursuing me. The Bible says, "The Lord is near to the brokenhearted and saves the crushed in spirit" (Psalm 34:18), and I am living proof of His unfailing love.

CHAPTER TWO

Street Life

"There is a way that seems right to a man, but its end is the way to death."

—Proverbs 14:12

The streets in the 1970s were their own world— raw, unforgiving, and full of temptations. For many Black men, the streets were both a means of survival and a trap, offering a false sense of power and freedom while leading to destruction. I was no exception. My life during that time revolved around what people now call the "hustle." I was deeply entrenched in street life, doing things that seemed normal then but that I now recognize as a path far from God.

The Allure of the Streets

Growing up, I was drawn to the idea of being my own boss, of not answering to anyone but myself. For Black men in the '70s, success was often defined by how much respect you commanded on the streets, how much money you had, and what you drove. Cadillac was the ultimate status symbol—a big deal for us. If you had a Cadillac, you weren't just surviving; you were living.

The streets promised a kind of freedom that society denied us. But that freedom came with a cost. My involvement in the "street life" led me down a path of drug use by the age of 16, and a lifestyle centered around crime. It was a vicious cycle: fast money, fast women, and fast living. It all seemed glamorous at the time, but it was a façade.

The Man of Leisure

I embraced the lifestyle of a "man of leisure," which in street terms meant I wasn't tied to a 9-to-5. I was my own boss, hustling to make money in ways that didn't always align with the law. I got into pimping—a world that seemed like easy money but was full of darkness. I thought I was in control, but looking back, I realize that the streets were controlling me.

There was an unspoken code in the lifestyle—a way to dress, a way to talk, and a way to carry yourself. Cadillac wasn't just a car; it was a statement. The sharp suits, the jewelry, the shoes—they were all part of the image. It was a way of saying, "I've made it," even if deep down, I was lost.

Addictions and Vices

"For all that is in the world—the desires of the flesh and the desires of the eyes and pride of life— is not from the Father but is from the world."
—1 John 2:16

The lifestyle wasn't just about money and cars. It was fueled by drugs, alcohol, and other vices. What started as casual use turned into an obsession. Drugs weren't just a way to escape reality—they became reality. Guns and violence were always present, either as a means of protection or as a tool for power.

I was reckless, and it was only by God's grace that I survived. The drugs clouded my judgment, the alcohol numbed my pain, and the crime created more problems than it ever solved. The streets gave me temporary highs, but they couldn't fill the emptiness inside.

The Fall

"Whoever conceals his transgressions will not prosper, but he who confesses and forsakes them will obtain mercy."—Proverbs 28:13

Eventually, the streets caught up with me. I ended up in jail, a harsh wake-up call that forced me to confront the reality of my choices. Sitting behind bars, I had a lot of time to think. I thought about the people I've hurt, the time wasted, and the man I had become. The obsession with Cadillacs, with status, with power—it all seemed so meaningless when I was stripped of everything.

Jail was a turning point, though I didn't realize it at the time. It was the beginning of the end of my street life and the start of a new chapter, though it would take years for me to fully turn my life around.

Looking Back

Now, as I reflect on that time, I see how God's hand was on me even when I didn't acknowledge Him. He kept me alive when so many others didn't make it. The street life promised freedom but delivered bondage. It promised power but left me powerless. It promised fulfillment but left me empty.

Those experiences are a reminder of where I came from and how far God has brought me. I don't share this to glorify the streets but to show that no matter how deep you are in, God can pull you out. I'm living proof that His grace is sufficient.

CHAPTER THREE

The Game You Play

"Do not be deceived: god is not mocked,
for whatever one sows, that will he
also reap." —Galatians 6:7

Life in the streets was chaotic, fast-paced, and filled with twisted dynamics. When I reflect on the relationship with my ex-wife, Mary, it's hard not to see how the chaos of the street life bled into our marriage. What began as a partnership based on love—or at least something like it—quickly became another extension of the hustle.

The Barber Shop Revelation

I'll never forget that conversation in the barber shop. It was a casual day, and I wasn't expecting my life to take the turn it did. Another pimp in the shop casually dropped the bomb: "Your wife is the best hoe out here." At first, I was taken aback. But the way he said it—with a mixture of respect and knowing—made me pause. He wasn't insulting me; he was giving advice. He told me she should be my main chick, my top earner.

I thought about it on my way home. I already had four women working for me, and I was deep into that life. The idea didn't seem as outrageous as it should have. Fueled by drugs and the toxic environment I was living in, I made a decision that changed everything.

Turning My Wife Out

That weekend, high on heroin, I drove up to our apartment and asked Mary to get dressed. I told her we were going somewhere. She didn't ask too many questions, but I could sense she knew something was up. I drove her to a spot where I often worked with my other girls.

When we arrived, I told her flat out: "You either do this, or you can go." The words hung in the air. I drove around the block, giving her time to process. My mind was clouded, but I convinced myself that this was just another move in the pimping game for me.

When I returned, I saw her standing on the corner, crying. She wasn't built for this life, and deep down, I knew it. A part of me felt guilty, but I pushed it down. One of the other girls came up to me and said Mary wasn't working. I drove back, picked Mary up, and took her home.

The Breaking Point

After dropping her off, I went back to the streets and collected my money from the other women. When I returned home, everything seemed quiet. I thought the drama was over, but when I got out of the shower, she was gone. It was around Christmas, and her leaving felt like a slap in the face.

A few days later, my phone rang. It was a call from Greensboro, Alabama. Mary was on the line, and she told me she couldn't do this anymore—not unless I changed. I wasn't ready to change, so I let her go.

Moving On Without Her

I didn't dwell on Mary's departure for long. I moved the other women into the apartment and appointed

Elaine as the new "main chick." She had the keys, and I trusted her to keep things running smoothly. I told myself everything was fine. Business was good, and my mom was even helping me pick out a new Eldorado Cadillac. She missed her granddaughter Latasha, and I made sure to let her spend time with the baby, even though I was spiraling deeper into my lifestyle.

The Back-and-Forth

Mary and I stayed in touch, though our conversations were full of tension. She moved to New York, and I told her I wanted her to come back. She didn't believe I had changed, and truthfully, I hadn't. Eventually, I drove to New York, took the baby, and left her behind. She called me before I left the city, saying she wanted to come back, but I told her to catch the next bus.

When she returned, I dropped her and the baby off at my mom's house. Mary later asked to move back in with me, but by then, I had moved Elaine into the apartment. Mary stayed for a few months, but it was clear things weren't going to work. She left again, for good.

The Fire

While Mary was gone, one of the girls left a space heater on, and the apartment caught fire. The apartment building that my father allowed me and the girls to live in. It was another low point in my life, but by then, I was used to picking up the pieces. My father never said anything about the incident, and I didn't have to pay for the damages. I just moved into another apartment on St. Clair and kept things moving.

A Toxic Cycle

My life during this time was a whirlwind of drama, money, and manipulation. Mary and I were separated, and my mom was raising our daughter. The women in my life were constantly dying for my attention and position. My main girl, Elaine, started to stand out, collecting money and showing her dominance. The other girls grew jealous, and the tension was always bubbling beneath the surface.

Reflection

Looking back, it's clear that the lifestyle I was living wasn't sustainable. I treated people as commodities, including my own wife. The choices I made during this time were driven by greed, addiction, and a warped sense of power. The fire, the back-and-forth with Mary, and the constant chaos were all signs that my life was out of control.

God was trying to get my attention, but I wasn't ready to listen. The streets had a hold on me, and I was too blinded by the game to see the damage I was causing— to myself, to Mary, and to everyone around me.

CHAPTER FOUR

God Calling Me

"Come to me, all you who are weary and burdened, and i will give you rest."

—Matthew 11:28

There comes a time when even the hardest pimp grows weary of the game. The fast money, the drama, the danger—all of it becomes too heavy. Deep down, I knew the life I was living wasn't sustainable. It was as if something was gnawing at my soul, whispering that I couldn't keep running forever. That whisper was God, but it took a life-altering moment for me to finally listen.

Weary of the Game

The streets had taken their toll on me and I charged them. The grind wasn't as exciting as it used to be, and the weight of my decisions was catching up with me. My main girl Elaine left and went to another "man of leisure" and wanted to come back, but she couldn't be trusted; that was the ultimate betrayal. An augment took place and I wound up getting stabbed in my leg by Elaine. I got my gun and I was about seven feet away from her. I had God on one shoulder, and the devil on the other. Things were happening so fast the devil was showing me the streets and God was showing me flashes of my life and telling me not to do it. I pulled the trigger anyway and God was protecting me because none of the bullets killed her. My boy had grabbed me and a wild shot caught her in the foot. And I had to go to the hospital because of my stab wound. My mother came to pray for me, and even though I was stubborn and still clinging to my old ways, I felt the power of her prayers. She told me, "God has His hand on you, even now. You can't keep running forever."

This was the start of God working on softening my heart.

The Night Everything Changed

The night I got shot was another turning point. It started like any other night—me out in the streets, handling business. I wasn't expecting trouble, but trouble has a way of finding you when you live in the street life. A confrontation escalated with my cousin and I. My cousin was a Preacher. I asked him "What was the difference between a Preacher and a Pimp?" I felt how he was getting money from the "church members" was no different in how I was getting my money. That is where the argument began, and before

I knew it, I was hit. My cousin, the Preacher, shot me and almost killed me!

In those moments, lying there bleeding, everything slowed down. I felt a strange calm, almost like time itself paused. It wasn't fear or panic that overtook me—it was a sense of clarity. I could feel the presence of something greater than myself. I knew I was at a crossroads, and it felt as if God Himself was giving me a choice: keep going down this path and lose everything, or surrender and let Him guide me.

The Encounter

While I was recovering, I couldn't shake the experience. It was as though God was speaking directly to my spirit, saying, "It's time." Time to walk away from the life I had built, the life that was killing me. Time to stop running from Him.

I started thinking about all the times I had been spared—times when I should have been dead, in prison, or lost to addiction. It became clear to me that I hadn't survived by luck; I had survived by grace and my mother's prayers. God had been protecting me, even when I didn't deserve it, even when I wasn't looking for Him.

Salvation Experience

One night, not long after I was back on my feet, I found myself alone, reflecting on everything I had been through. The weight of my choices, the pain I had caused others, and the emptiness of the life I was living hit me all at once. I first went to my mother's house at 8am. She was asleep in the bed and I laid next to her. She woke up and asked me, What was wrong? I was crying and shaking. She thought I was "dope sick" but I wasn't. She offered me money. I told her

"No". I am tired of "The Life" and I can't do it any more, I-need-help!

I then fell to my knees and cried out to God. I didn't know the right words to say, but my heart was open. I told Him I was tired, that I couldn't do it on my own anymore. I asked Him to forgive me, to take control of my life, to make me new.

In that very moment, I felt something I had never felt before: peace. It was like a weight had been lifted off my shoulders. I knew I wasn't alone anymore. I knew I had been saved.

A New Beginning

The journey didn't end there—it was only the beginning. Walking away from the life I had built wasn't easy. There were temptations, setbacks, and people who didn't believe I had truly changed. But I clung to my salvation experience, to the memory of that night when God called me out of darkness and into His light.

God's call wasn't just about saving me from the streets; it was about saving me for something greater. He had a purpose for my life, and though I didn't fully understand it at the time, I knew I had to trust Him.

Reflection

Looking back, I realize that God had been calling me for years. He had planted seeds through the people I encountered, through the moments of grace that kept me alive, and even through the weariness I felt in my spirit.

Getting shot wasn't the end—it was the beginning of a new chapter, a chapter where God would take the broken pieces of my life and use them for His glory.

CHAPTER FIVE

Turning From Darkness to Light — Con- Artist Ex- Wife

"For you were once darkness, but now you are light in the Lord. Live as children of light." —Ephesians 5:8

As I reflect on my teenage years and young adulthood, I can see now how far I had drifted from the path God had for me. It wasn't that I didn't know better—I had grown up hearing about Jesus, sitting in church pews, and even dreaming about being a preacher. But the streets, the lifestyle, and the promise of quick money seemed more exciting than the quiet life of faith my mother always prayed I would follow.

Caught in the Darkness

"The way of the unfaithful is hard."
—Proverbs 13:15

When I look back, I realize how hard life was back then, even though I didn't admit it to myself at the time. My choices took me down a road that led to trouble after trouble. I remember stealing purses, breaking into homes, and even the time I nearly got shot and was shot because of my actions. That life might have seemed glamorous from the outside, but the truth is, it was empty and dangerous.

It wasn't long before I became trapped in that world. The people around me were caught up in the same lifestyle, and instead of lifting each other up, we dragged each other further down. I was blinded by the temporary excitement of money, women, and power. I didn't see the chains I was putting on my own life.

Through it all, my mother never stopped praying for me. She knew the man I could become, even when I couldn't see it myself. She would remind me of the Word of God and tell me, "Son, you were made for something greater." I didn't listen at the time, but her words stayed with me.

A Pivotal Moment

"If we confess our sins, He is faithful and just to forgive us our sins and to cleanse us from all unrighteousness." —1 John 1:9

There were many turning points in my life, but two were the most significant was when I found myself sitting in a jail cell doing 3-15 years for Compelling Prostitution. While I was in jail I was trying to kick my drug habit.. I had lost everything—my money, my so-called friends, and my freedom. It was just me and my thoughts. For the first time in a long time, I started to think about the life I was living and where it was leading me.

Second Wife- The Con Artist

After serving my time I got out early in November of 1984. I made a vow to stay away from black women because that was where I felt all my trouble started. While talking to my Lady friend she invited me to a New Year Eve party to bring in 1985. Went to a house party together. We were drinking and having a good time when this white Lady in a black mink coat walked in and caught my eye.I went over to talk to her and I was pouring my life story into her lap and she began to get annoyed and walked away. I walked outside, took a deep breath, went back in and took my shot at her again. I introduced myself "hi my name is Danny what's yours" She told me her name was Net. We sat and talked the whole night. She already knew a little bit about me from other people; she just wanted me to come correct. When she was ready to leave she asked me if I was coming with her or not. I looked for the girl I came with, she was nowhere in sight and I left with Net.

Things moved very fast. We lived together for about three months then I noticed one day in March She was preparing to go to work and she was dressed very Sophisticated so I didn't ask questions. As she walked out the door I looked out the window and she got in the car with three other white women and drove off.

When she came back she tossed $4,000 on the bed and told me that she was better than 10 hoes, She then said "I heard you used to be a pimp and i wasn't pimping anymore". She took $1,000 and said I'll be right back.

I got excited. I called my mom and told her everything that just happened. She thought I was going back to the streets and tried to explain that it wasn't like that. After I hung up, Net returned and asked if I did blow. I said "yeah" and she laid the heroin out on the table. While getting high she told me what she did for a living. She was a drag player also known as a con-artist. Life was good. We got married and had my beautiful daughter Daniele in 1986. My so-called good life caught up with me because I started selling blow and got arrested the last time I served a year in jail. It was at that moment, I cried out to God. "Lord, if You're real, if You can hear me, please help me. I can't do this on my own anymore." It wasn't an immediate transformation, but that prayer planted a seed in my heart. I began to feel a tugging, a pulling toward something better, something more in. When I got out of the Net I was no longer together. but we are still cool.

Stepping Into the Light

"Therefore, if anyone is in Christ, he is a new creation; old things have passed away; behold, all things have become new." —2 Corinthians 5:17

When I got out of jail, I knew I couldn't keep going back to the same people and the same lifestyle. My mother gave me a Bible and told me to start reading the Gospels. She said, "Son, you need to know who Jesus is for yourself." So, I did. I started with the book of Matthew, and for the first time, I felt like the words were speaking directly to me. After about a week or two my mother told me that it was time for me to leave her house and get back on my feet. So I left that night and found myself over my Indian Hills apartments. I cried out to the Lord asking him what my next steps were. He led me over to St. Clair and ran into an old friend who gave me the number to my old friend Gwen. I called her and we started talking and she invited me to stay with her that night.She lived over on Mayfield around the corner from New Spirit Revival Center. I got a job working at the UH hospital cleaning team. I started listening to church radio and reading my work. A pastor Darrell Scott radio station started talking about pimps. I called to check in to tell him that he was wrong and he asked me a question and asked me who I was and he asked my name and said he wanted to meet me. The next Sunday I showed up at church and shared my story and we built a mutual respect for each other.

I began attending church again, not just to please my mother, but because I wanted to know God for myself. It wasn't easy at first. The enemy kept trying to pull me back into my old ways, but every time I felt tempted, I remembered the promises of God. He said He would never leave me nor forsake me (Hebrews 13:5), and I held on to that.

CHAPTER SIX

Called to the Ministry

"And I heard the voice of the Lord

saying, 'Whom shall I send, and who will

go for us?' Then I said, 'Here I am!

Send me.'" —Isaiah 6:8

When I reflect on my journey into ministry, I am reminded of how patient and faithful God is. He doesn't just call the equipped; He equips the called. I didn't feel worthy of the calling on my life, but God used every mistake, every trial, and every triumph to prepare me for the work He had planned.

Hearing the Call

"Before I formed you in the womb I knew you, before you were born I set you apart; I appointed you as a prophet to the nations." —Jeremiah 1:5

After rededicating my life to Christ, I began to feel a stirring in my spirit. It started as a whisper during prayer or a verse that seemed to jump off the page when I read the Bible. I couldn't shake the feeling that God was calling me to do more than just sit in a pew. It was as if He was saying, "You've experienced My grace and mercy. Now, I want you to share it with others."

At first, I pushed the thought aside. I told myself I wasn't good enough. After all, I had a past—a long list of mistakes that I thought disqualified me. But God kept reminding me of His Word: "If anyone is in Christ, he is a new creation" (2 Corinthians 5:17). My past wasn't a barrier; it was a testimony of His power to transform.

Stepping Out in Faith

"For we are His workmanship, created in Christ Jesus for good works, which God prepared beforehand that we should walk in them."
—Ephesians 2:10

The first time I shared my testimony in church, I was terrified. I didn't think anyone would want to hear from someone like me. But as I spoke, I saw how God was using my story to touch others. People came up to me afterward, tears in their eyes, saying, "I've been there too," or, "If God can do that for you, maybe He can do it for me."

That moment was a turning point. I realized that ministry wasn't about being perfect; it was about being obedient. It wasn't about my qualifications; it was about His calling.

Training for the Work

"Study to show yourself approved unto God, a workman that needs not to be ashamed, rightly dividing the word of truth." —2 Timothy 2:15

I knew that if I was going to serve God effectively, I needed to equip myself. I started attending Bible study regularly and enrolled in ministerial training courses offered by my church. I learned how to rightly divide the Word of truth, how to counsel others, and how to lead with integrity.

There were times when I felt overwhelmed. Balancing work, family, and ministry was no easy task, but God's grace sustained me. I leaned on Philippians 4:13: "I can do all things through Christ who strengthens me." Every lesson, every challenge was shaping me into the servant God wanted me to be.

First Steps in Ministry

"Go therefore and make disciples of all nations, baptizing them in the name of the Father and of the Son and of the Holy Spirit." —Matthew 28:19

My first ministry role was serving as a deacon in training. It was humbling to assist in the practical needs of the church, from setting up for services to visiting the sick. I saw firsthand how ministry wasn't just about preaching—it was about serving.

From there, God opened doors for me to lead Bible studies and speak at youth events. I felt a deep burden for young men who were caught in the same traps I had once fallen into. I wanted them to know there was a way out, that Jesus could give them a new identity and purpose.

A New Mission

"But seek first the kingdom of God and His righteousness, and all these things shall be added to you." —Matthew 6:33

Over time, God began to open doors for me. I started serving in the church, and eventually became a deacon in training. It was a complete turnaround from the life I had been living. I went from someone who took from others to someone who wanted to give back.

One of the most beautiful things was meeting Angel, the woman who would become my wife. She saw me for who I was becoming, not who I had been. Her love and support were like a confirmation from God that I was on the right path.

Looking Ahead

"Let us not grow weary in doing good, for at the proper time we will reap a harvest if we do not give up." —Galatians 6:9

Today, I am more committed than ever to the work of the Lord. I know there are still challenges ahead, but I also know that God is faithful. He has brought me this far, and I trust Him to lead me the rest of the way.

CHAPTER SEVEN

The Third is a Charm – My Good Thing

"He who finds a wife finds a good thing

and obtains favor from the lord."

—Proverbs 18:22

They say the third time's the charm, and in my case, it couldn't be more true. My wife, Angel Hunter, is my good thing—the woman God sent into my life to show me what true love, partnership, and grace look like. After all the pain, mistakes, and lessons learned, Angel has been the blessing I never knew I needed.

A Love Built on God

Angel and I have been married for nine years now, and what a journey it has been. When I look back on my life, it's nothing short of a miracle that God brought someone like her into my world. She knows everything about my past—the good, the bad, and the downright ugly. Yet she loves me anyway. She didn't just accept my story; she embraced it, understanding that it's part of what makes me who I am today.

Together, we've built a life centered on faith. We bought a house, a home that represents stability and growth—something I thought I would never have. We serve together in ministry at New Beginning

Ministries, pouring into the same community that has poured into us. Having Angel by my side in both life and ministry is a constant reminder of God's grace and His ability to redeem even the most broken parts of our lives.

Ups and Downs, But Always Love

Like any couple, we've had our ups and downs. Marriage isn't always easy, but it's always worth it. What I love most about Angel is her ability to love unconditionally, even when I fall short. She has a strength that inspires me and a faith that keeps me grounded.

When things get tough, we lean on the foundation we've built together—a foundation rooted in God. We pray together, seek counsel when needed, and strive to grow not just as a couple but as individuals walking in our God-given purpose.

The Gift of Godly Examples

One of the greatest blessings in our marriage has been the example set by Apostle Greg and Prophet Teresa McCurry. Watching them navigate life and ministry as a couple has been invaluable. They don't just preach about love and unity; they live it every day. Their marriage is a reflection of what it means to love God and each other wholeheartedly.

Chief Apostle Greg's wisdom and strength combined with Prophet Tee's nurturing spirit and fiery passion for God are a perfect balance. They show us what it means to communicate, to forgive, and to serve one another selflessly. Having their mentorship has been like having a blueprint for what a Godly marriage looks like.

Angel and I often talk about how blessed we are to have such a strong example before us. It's a reminder that marriage isn't just about love—it's about partnership, purpose, and ministry.

Thankful Every Day

Every day, I thank God for Angel. She's not just my wife; she's my partner, my confidant, my prayer warrior, and my best friend. She has been a source of healing and hope in my life, showing me what it truly means to be loved by someone who sees you the way God does—with grace and mercy.

Our story is a testament to God's redemption and His ability to take what was broken and make it beautiful. Angel is my "good thing," and through her, I've learned to love better, live better, and walk in the purpose God has for me.

CHAPTER EIGHT

In The Game in the Church

"No one can serve two masters. Either you will hate the one and love the other, or you will be devoted to the one and despise the other." —Matthew 6:24

My sister Terrie invited me to a new church on the westside and I really enjoyed it. I started to go to the church and I started to share my life with Chief Apostle Mccurry (formerly Pastor McCurry) and I told him how I felt about the churches and pastors. I explained to him that I am putting my trust in you and if he ever crossed me, I would fuck him up.

He looked at me and said, "You can Trust Me", and we hugged each other. To this day he has shown me nothing but love. He loved me, accepted me and everything opened up for me and my wife.

Later I met Prophet Tearea, his wife whom I knew when she was younger. Funny how life became a full circle. I have been a faithful member at New Beginning Ministries ever since and have not turned back. Pastor McCurry, now Chief Apostle McCurry, is still standing on her word for me to trust him.

New Beginnings

Things began to change when I found myself at New Beginning Ministries. Walking into that church was like walking into a new life. For the first time, I started to see the world differently. It wasn't just about survival anymore; it was about purpose.

The teachings at New Beginning hit differently. The Word of God was broken down in a way that made sense to me, that resonated with where I was in my life. When Pastor Teresa—affectionately known as Pastor Tee—preached, it felt like she was speaking directly to me. She wasn't just talking about God; she was showing me how to live for Him in a real and practical way.

Pastor Tee played a huge role in helping me understand what that meant. She didn't just preach at me; she discipled me. She took the time to explain my calling and my purpose. She showed me how to align my life with God's will, and for the first time, I began to truly understand what it meant to walk with the Lord.

She taught me that my past didn't disqualify me from God's purpose. In fact, it was part of my testimony—

part of the story God wanted to use to reach others who were still trapped in the life I had left behind.

Her mentorship was life-changing. She didn't sugarcoat the truth, and she didn't let me make excuses. She challenged me to be better, to grow, and to fully commit to my faith. Through her guidance, the light bulb finally came on. I realized I couldn't keep playing both sides. I had to choose.

Ordained by God

"And He Himself gave some to be apostles, some prophets, some evangelists, and some pastors and teachers, for the equipping of the saints for the work of ministry." —Ephesians 4:11-12

My turning point came when I was ordained as a deacon. It wasn't just a title or a role—it was a responsibility, a call to step up and live the life God had been calling me to all along. That ordination wasn't about recognition; it was about transformation. It was as if God was saying, "You're not who you used to be anymore. I've called you to something greater."

The day I was ordained as a minister was one of the most humbling and joyful moments of my life. Standing before the congregation, with my wife and children by my side, I felt the weight of the calling— but also the assurance that God would guide me every step of the way.

As the elders laid hands on me and prayed, I felt the presence of the Holy Spirit in a way I never had before. It was as if God was confirming, "This is what I made you for." I promised that day to serve Him with all my heart, to preach His Word faithfully, and to love His people as He loves them.

One of the most rewarding parts of ministry has been seeing lives changed. Watching someone come to the altar, broken and lost, and leave filled with the peace and joy of Christ reminds me why I do what I do. It's not about me; it's all about Him.

Getting Serious About My Walk

Once I got serious about my walk with the Lord, everything began to shift. The Word of God became more than just something I heard on Sunday mornings—it became the foundation of my life. I started to see the fruits of living in obedience to God.

It wasn't easy, though. The pull of the streets didn't just disappear overnight, and there were moments when I was tempted to go back. But the more I leaned into God's Word, the more I realized I didn't need the streets to define me anymore.

Reflection

Being "in the game" in the church was a tug-of-war between two worlds. It took time, patience, and a lot of grace for me to fully surrender to God's plan for my life. But once I did, I discovered a freedom and a purpose that the streets could never offer.

Now, I can see how God used every step of my journey—the good, the bad, and the ugly—to bring me to where I am today. He didn't just call me out of the world; He called me into His Kingdom, and that changed everything.

CHAPTER NINE

Finding my Voice in Ministry

"For the gifts and the calling of God are

irrevocable." —Romans 11:29

One of the most defining moments in my ministry journey was when I stepped out to teach my first Bible study for NBM's Bible Study. It was an opportunity that excited me but also filled me with nerves. The Word of God is powerful, and I wanted to handle it correctly, to bless others and glorify Him.

The First Attempt: A Valuable Lesson

"Every way of a man is right in his own eyes, but the Lord weighs the heart." —Proverbs 21:2

As a deacon it was my turn to teach Bible Study. Pastor Al Jackson was gracious in preparing me for the lesson. He worked tirelessly with me, showing me his style, structure, and approach to delivering a Bible study. I admired his depth of knowledge and his ability to connect with people through Scripture. Naturally, I tried to follow his example. I carefully prepared my notes, laid everything out in his format, and practiced until I felt ready.

But when the moment came to teach, things didn't go as planned. I stumbled through the lesson, and it felt awkward and disjointed. The harder I tried to stick to his structure, the more things seemed to unravel. While teaching the Bible Study lesson on Zoom, I lost my internet connection. As a result I didn't complete my assignment. My heart was in the right place, but it didn't flow.

Looking back, I realized that while I was trying to honor God, I wasn't fully being myself. God had gifted me with my own personality, style, and way of teaching His Word. Trying to imitate someone else wasn't what He wanted from me.

A New Approach: Trusting God's Design

"Do not neglect the gift you have... Practice these things, immerse yourself in them, so that all may see your progress." —1 Timothy 4:14-15

The next time I had the opportunity to teach, Prophet Teresa McCurry—my spiritual mother—stepped in. She sat with me and encouraged me to come as myself. She said, "Let the Lord use you in your unique flavor. Don't try to be anyone else. Trust that He will speak through you."

Her advice was like a breath of fresh air. I prepared my lesson in a way that felt authentic to who I was. Instead of trying to follow a rigid format, I prayed for guidance and let the Scriptures speak to me. I focused on connecting with the attendees, sharing not only the Word but also how it applied to my life and could apply to theirs.

When God Took Over

"Now to Him who is able to do far more abundantly than all that we ask or think, according to the power at work within us."
—Ephesians 3:20

That second Bible study was a completely different experience. As I started teaching, the Holy Spirit took over. The words flowed naturally, and the Scriptures came alive in a way that was both exciting and humbling. It felt like I was having a conversation with the attendees, walking with them through the Word, rather than just presenting information.

The attendees were engaged, asking questions and sharing their insights. The lesson not only blessed them but also me. Time seemed to fly, and before I knew it, we had gone over the scheduled time—but no one seemed to mind. Afterward, people reached out to say how much the lesson had impacted them, and I was reminded that when we yield to God, He truly does the work through us.

Rediscovering My Focus

"But seek first the kingdom of God and His righteousness, and all these things will be added to you." —Matthew 6:33

That experience taught me two crucial lessons. First, ministry is about authenticity—being who God created me to be and trusting Him to work through that. Second, the best ministry happens when I'm focused on Him.

I'll admit that life has distractions, and sometimes I lose sight of the calling. There are moments when I find myself caught up in the busyness of life, letting my attention drift from the things of God. But that Bible study was a reminder of the joy and fulfillment that comes from walking in obedience to Him. It reignited my passion for ministry and encouraged me to keep pursuing the work He has for me.

Moving Forward: Walking in Purpose

"Commit your work to the Lord, and your plans will be established." —Proverbs 16:3

As I look ahead, I know I need to refocus and fully commit to the things of God. The world is full of distractions, but there's nothing more important than fulfilling the purpose He's given me. I'm reminded of the power of community—of spiritual mentors like Prophet Teresa McCurry and leaders like Pastor Al Jackson—who help guide me back to the path when I stray.

I want to walk forward with the same faith and passion I felt during that second Bible study, trusting God to use me in His way and in His timing. It's not about perfection; it's about obedience and reliance on His strength.

CHAPTER TEN

※☆※

My New Beginning

"Therefore, if anyone is in Christ, the new creation has come: the old has gone, the new is here!"— 2 Corinthians 5:17

There's a song that says, "I have decided to follow Jesus, no turning back." That's the kind of life I want to live. But if I'm being honest, the streets still try to call my name. Temptation doesn't just vanish because you give your life to Christ—it's a fight every day. Still, I know I'm not the man I used to be. God has saved me, filled me with His Holy Spirit, and set me on a new path.

A New Beginning, but Not an Easy Road

When I reflect on my life, I see God's hand guiding me through every twist and turn. Even in my darkest moments, He was calling me, waiting for me to surrender. But stepping into a new life hasn't been easy. It's like leaving behind a part of yourself that's been with you for years. The streets are familiar. They have a way of making you feel powerful, in control. But it's all an illusion.

Now, I know that true power comes from God. True control is giving your life over to Him and trusting His plan. When I struggle, I remind myself of who I am now: a man saved by grace, a servant of God, and a witness to His power to transform lives.

Salvation and the Evidence of the Holy Spirit

One of the most significant moments in my faith journey was receiving the Holy Spirit. It wasn't just a church experience—it was personal. I felt God's presence in a way I never had before. It gave me strength, clarity, and the conviction to pursue a life that honors Him.

The Holy Spirit helps me fight the pull of the streets. When temptation comes, I lean on prayer, scripture, and the teachings of my church leaders. I've learned that I can't do this alone. But with God, all things are possible.

Reflections on My Christian Upbringing

My journey started long before I realized it. Growing up, church was a part of my life, even if I didn't always take it seriously. My mom introduced me to faith in her own way. She believed in God but struggled to provide for us. Her words planted seeds in me, even though some of her actions and advice led me astray.

She used to tell me, "I can't provide for you like your sisters." That statement shaped me. It made me believe I had to fend for myself, even if it meant manipulating women to get what I wanted. I learned how to use charm and persuasion to survive, but I see now that it was all a façade.

Manipulating women meant exploiting their feelings for my own gain. I'd make them feel special, needed, and wanted, all while using them to get what I wanted—whether it was money, status, or control. It's a hard truth to admit, but it's part of my story.

Finding Redemption and Purpose

What's amazing is that God doesn't hold our past against us. When I came to New Beginning Ministries, I truly found my new beginning. The teaching and mentorship I received there helped me understand God's love and my purpose in His plan.

Becoming a deacon and serving in ministry gave me a new sense of identity. It's not about what I can take from others anymore—it's about what I can give. Whether it's sharing my testimony, helping someone in need, or simply being present, I'm learning to live a life of service.

Looking Ahead

I'm still a work in progress. There are days when I struggle, when the streets seem louder than God's voice. But I've learned to tune my ear to Him. I focus on His promises, His grace, and the life He's called me to live.

This book is a testament to His power to redeem. It's about how He took a boy from the streets, a man lost in sin, and gave him a new name, a new purpose, and a new beginning.

To anyone reading this, my prayer is that you see yourself in this story—not in the mistakes, but in the possibility of redemption. No matter where you've been or what you've done, God's love is greater. He's calling you, just like He called me. All you have to do is say yes.

"Therefore, if anyone is in Christ, the new creation has come: The old has gone, the new is here!" — 2 Corinthians 5:17

There's a feeling that comes with truly surrendering to God—a sense of release, a sense of being made new. This scripture, 2 Corinthians 5:17, encapsulates the transformation I've experienced in my life. The old has gone, the new is here. And that has never been truer for me than it is right now.

A New Creation in Christ

When I first encountered Christ, it was as though a veil was lifted from my eyes. The world I once thought was everything suddenly looked empty, and the life I had built for myself seemed so far removed from the life God had designed for me. For so long, I had been living in the shadows of my past, convinced that I was bound to it forever. But when I gave my heart to God, I began to understand the true meaning of this scripture. I was not just forgiven; I was made new.

This new creation didn't mean I didn't still face struggles or that my past didn't try to creep back into my mind. But the power of God's love and grace was greater than anything I had ever known. The old ways of thinking, the old desires, the old mindset—it all began to fade as I learned to walk in the newness that only Christ could give.

Living with the Evidence of the Holy Spirit

Receiving the Holy Spirit was a turning point for me. The Holy Spirit didn't just come into my life as a nice idea or a comforting presence; He became my constant guide. He led me through the temptations, the doubts, and the moments where I felt like I might fall back into my old ways. It was the Holy Spirit's presence in me that helped me take the first steps of living out this new creation.

There are days when the streets call out to me, pulling me back to the life I used to know. But in those moments, I remember the truth of 2 Corinthians 5:17: I am no longer the man I was. The old me—the man of the streets, the man who used others for his own gain—he's gone. In his place is a new man, a man of purpose, a man with God's Spirit inside of him, leading him to walk in holiness.

The Power of Redemption and Change

One of the most significant moments of change for me came when I realized that I didn't have to stay in the life I had been living. I didn't have to let my past define me. I had been taught by my family and by my experiences that the streets were the only way, that manipulation and survival were my only options. But when I encountered God, I saw that He had a better way.

God's calling on my life was not to go back to what I knew, but to move forward in the new identity He had given me. I can now see my past not as something that defines me but as a testimony of God's grace. The things I once thought were unchangeable were erased by God's mercy, and in their place is a life marked by peace, purpose, and freedom.

Living Out My New Beginning

Being in ministry and serving at New Beginning Ministries has allowed me to live out this transformation in a tangible way. It's not enough just to believe that the old is gone; I had to live like it. Every day, I make the decision to let go of the old man and walk in the newness that Christ offers.

Through the teachings of Chief Apostle Greg & Prophet Teresa (Pastor Tee) and the support of those around me, I've come to understand my purpose. I've come to understand that being a new creation doesn't just mean I've been forgiven—it means I'm being shaped into something greater.

The old life is still calling me, but it no longer has power over me. Through the power of the Holy Spirit, I've been given the ability to resist temptation, to stand firm in my new identity, and to continue walking the path God has laid out for me.

A New Beginning, a New Hope

The most amazing part of this transformation is that it's not just for me—it's for anyone who chooses Christ. It doesn't matter what your past looks like, what you've done, or how many times you've fallen. God is in the business of making new creations.

When we surrender to Him, we get a fresh start. The old is gone, and the new is here.

As I reflect on the journey I've taken, I realize that my new beginning is not just about the change in me; it's about the hope I can offer others. If God can make a new creation out of me, He can do the same for anyone.

Prayer:

Father God, I thank You for making me a new creation in Christ. Thank You for forgiving me, for healing me, and for giving me a fresh start. I pray that Your Spirit continues to guide me and that I live my life as a reflection of Your grace and love. Help me to walk in the newness of life every day and to share that hope with those around me. In Jesus' name, Amen.

With LOVE and RESPECT

REDEEMED

From Pimp to Pulpit
"A Life Transformed By Grace"
R.E.D.E.E.M.E.D.

R – Restored: From a broken life to a purpose-filled existence.

E – Empowered: By faith to overcome the chains of the past.

D – Delivered: From the grip of sin and the streets.

E – Equipped: With the Word and Spirit to serve and inspire.

E – Elevated: To a new life of integrity and love.

M – Mentored: By spiritual leaders who modeled Godly living.

E – Embraced: By God's grace, mercy, and unconditional love.

D – Dedicated: To living out a divine purpose in service to others.

~ Deacon George (Danny) Hunter

About the Author

George (Danny) Hunter is a testament to the transformative power of grace, perseverance, and redemption. Born and raised in Cleveland, Ohio, he experienced the highs and lows of street life in the 1970s, navigating challenges, mistakes, and pivotal moments that would ultimately lead him to embrace his God-given purpose.

After years of living in the fast lane, Danny had a life-changing encounter with God that set him on a path of faith and renewal. Today, he serves in ministry at New Beginning Ministries alongside his wife, Angel, dedicating his life to helping others find hope, healing, and purpose through God's word.

As a proud husband, father, and grandfather, Danny is committed to showing how God's grace can rewrite even the most difficult stories. This book shares his incredible journey from the streets to the sanctuary—a testimony to the life-changing power of redemption.

McCurry Ministries
International Publishing
Assistance

Serving God's People, Telling Their Story

McCurry Ministries International Publishing Assistance (MMIPA) Firm

At MMIPA, we are an impact-driven author assistance and Self-publishing firm dedicated to empowering authors through branding and development services. Our mission is to guide writers in transforming their ideas into influential works, while enhancing their presence as thought leaders in their fields.

Founders

Teresa S. McCurry, CEO and President

Gregory McCurry, Vice President

Contact Us

Website: www.nbfellowshipint.org

Email: MMI.serving.people@gmail.com

Address: 2060 West 65th Street, Cleveland, Ohio 44102

www.ingramcontent.com/pod-product-compliance
Lightning Source LLC
Chambersburg PA
CBHW070003100426
42741CB00012B/3110